361 Full-Color Allover Patterns for Artists and Craftspeople

Selected and Arranged by
Carol Belanger Grafton

DOVER PUBLICATIONS, INC.
Mineola, New York

Bibliographical Note

361 Full-Color Allover Patterns for Artists and Craftspeople is a new work, first published by Dover Publications, Inc., in 1999.

DOVER *Pictorial Archive* SERIES

This book belongs to the Dover Pictorial Archive Series. You may use the designs and illustrations for graphics and crafts applications, free and without special permission, provided that you include no more than ten in the same publication or project. (For permission for additional use, please write to Permissions Department, Dover Publications, Inc., 31 East 2nd Street, Mineola, N.Y. 11501.)
However, republication or reproduction of any illustration by any other graphic service, whether it be in a book or in any other design resource, is strictly prohibited.

International Standard Book Number: 0-486-40268-1

Manufactured in the United States of America
Dover Publications, Inc., 31 East 2nd Street, Mineola, N.Y. 11501

Note

This book of full-color patterns is intended for anyone in need of copyright-free designs for use in art, craft, and other projects. The patterns have been selected for their beauty, variety, and practicality and have been painstakingly reproduced from many sources (a list of which appears on p. 91) including rare books and portfolios. Styles range from Ancient Egyptian to Victorian, Amish to Art Deco. This archive is an invaluable source of designs for direct permission-free use and an excellent reference for design inspiration as well.

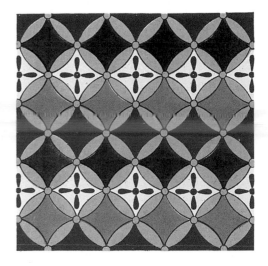

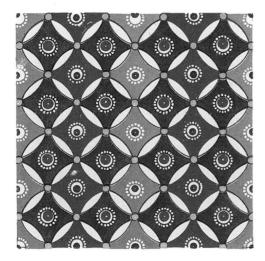

1

4

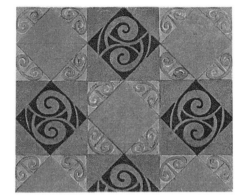

12

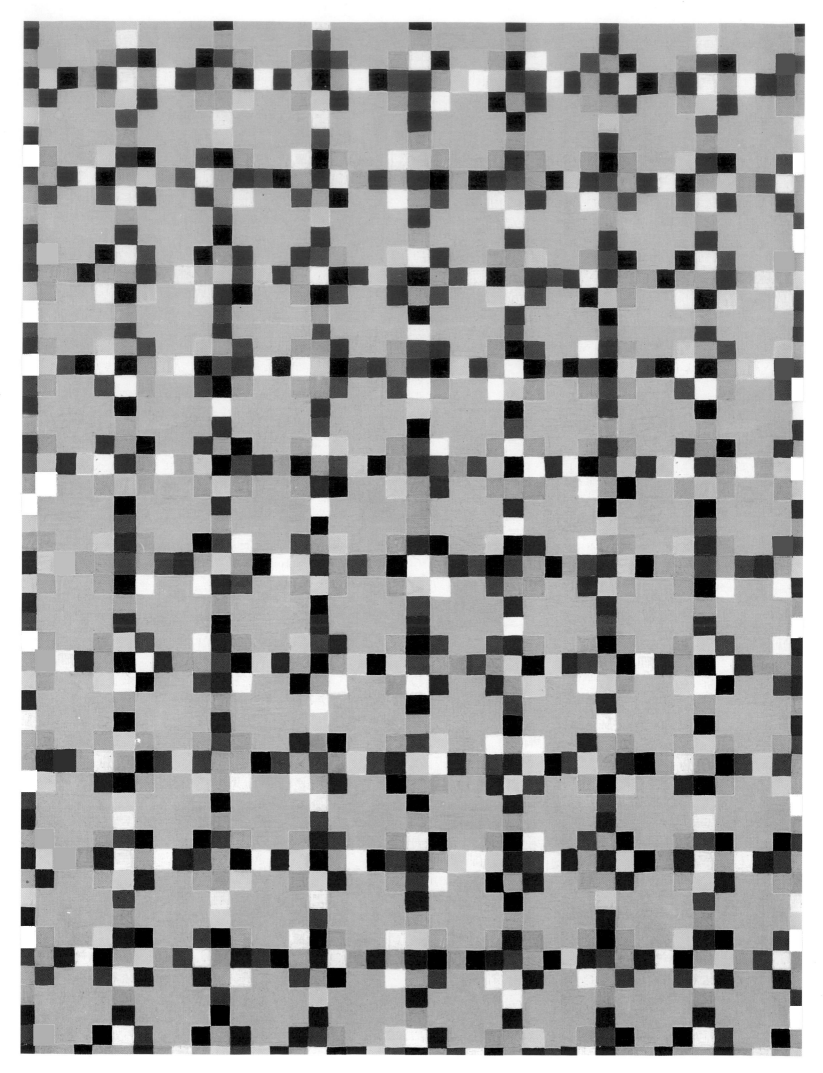

14

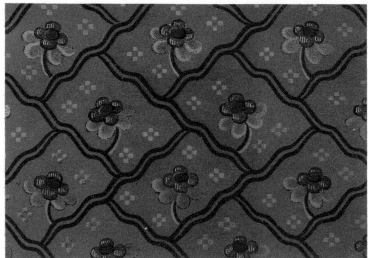

17

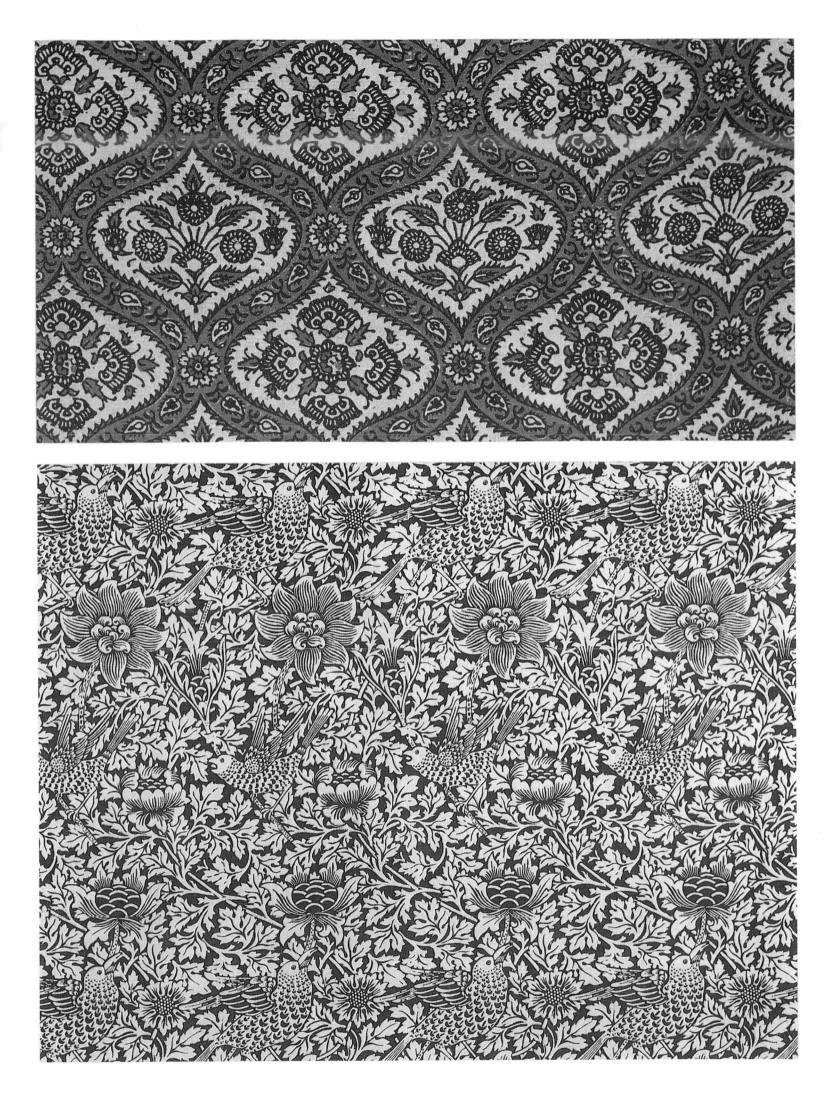

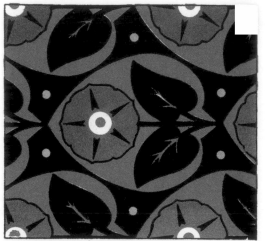

 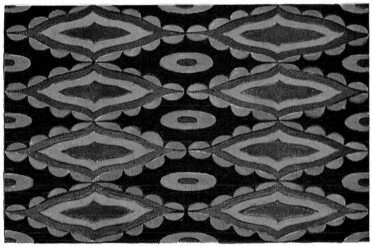

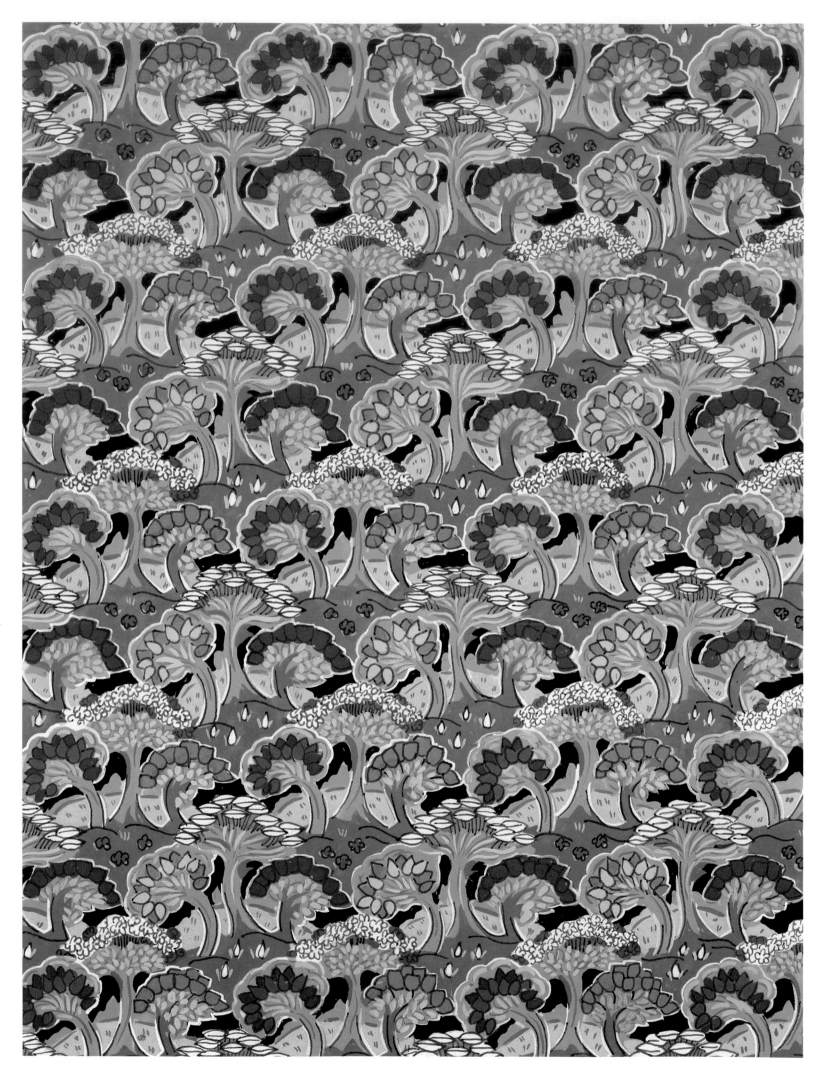

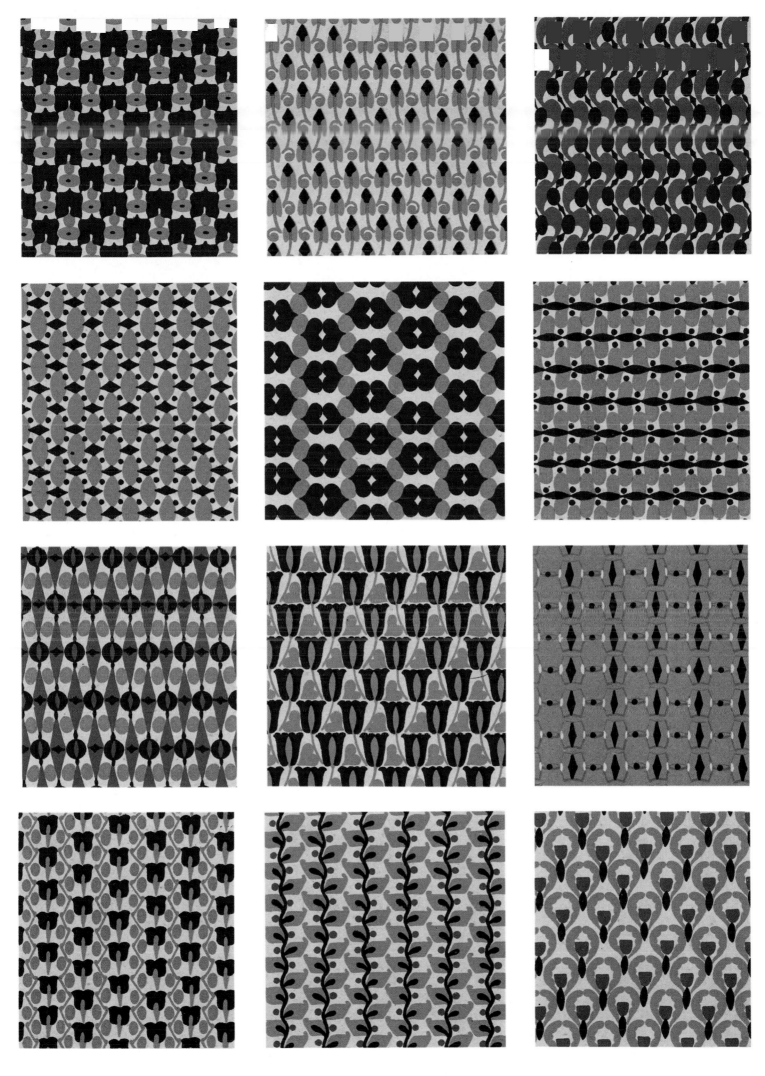

32

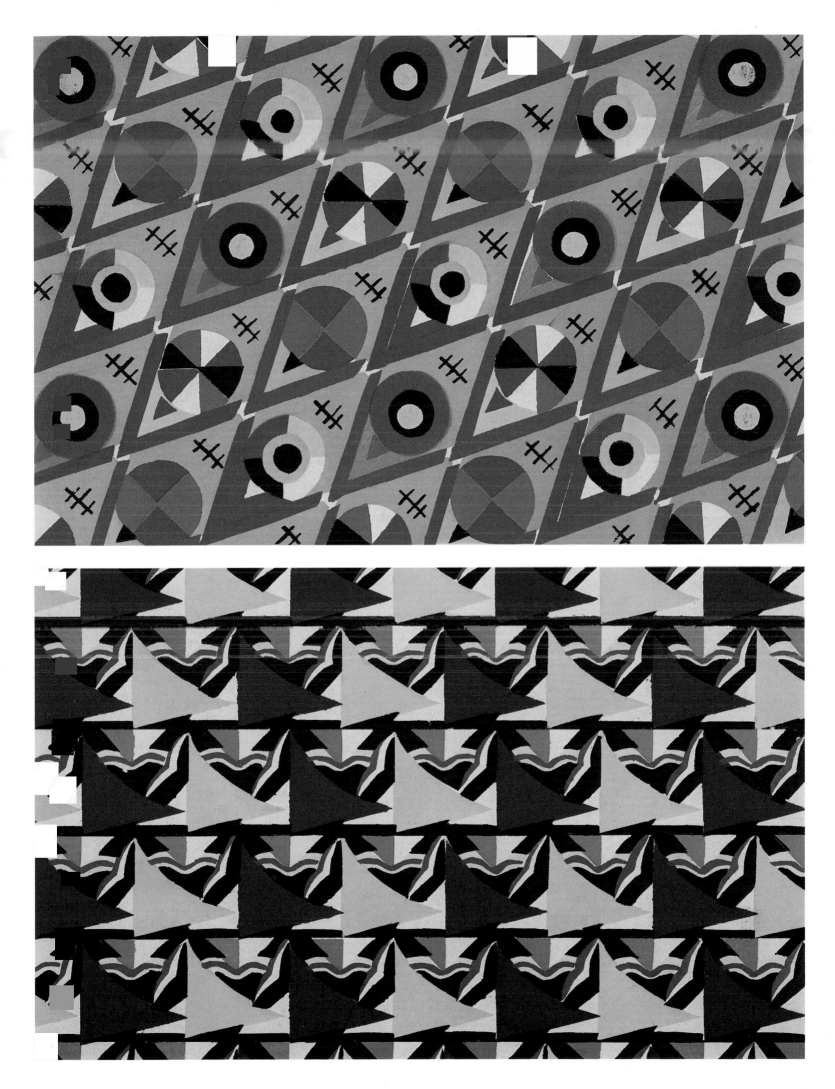

33

36

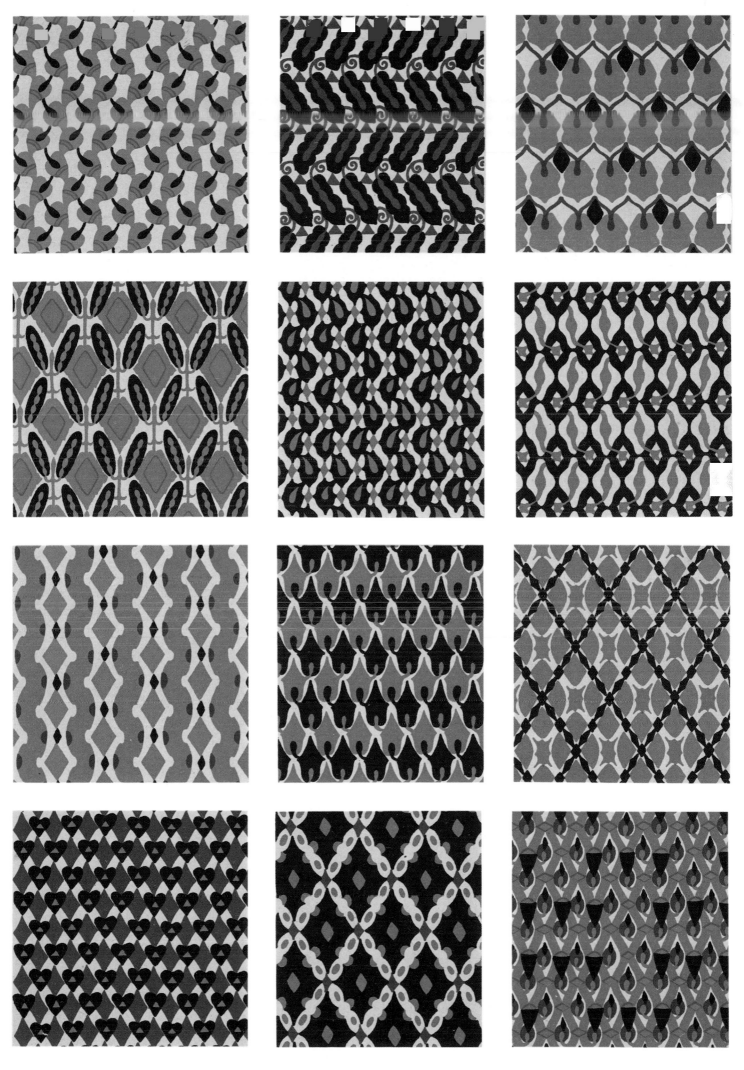

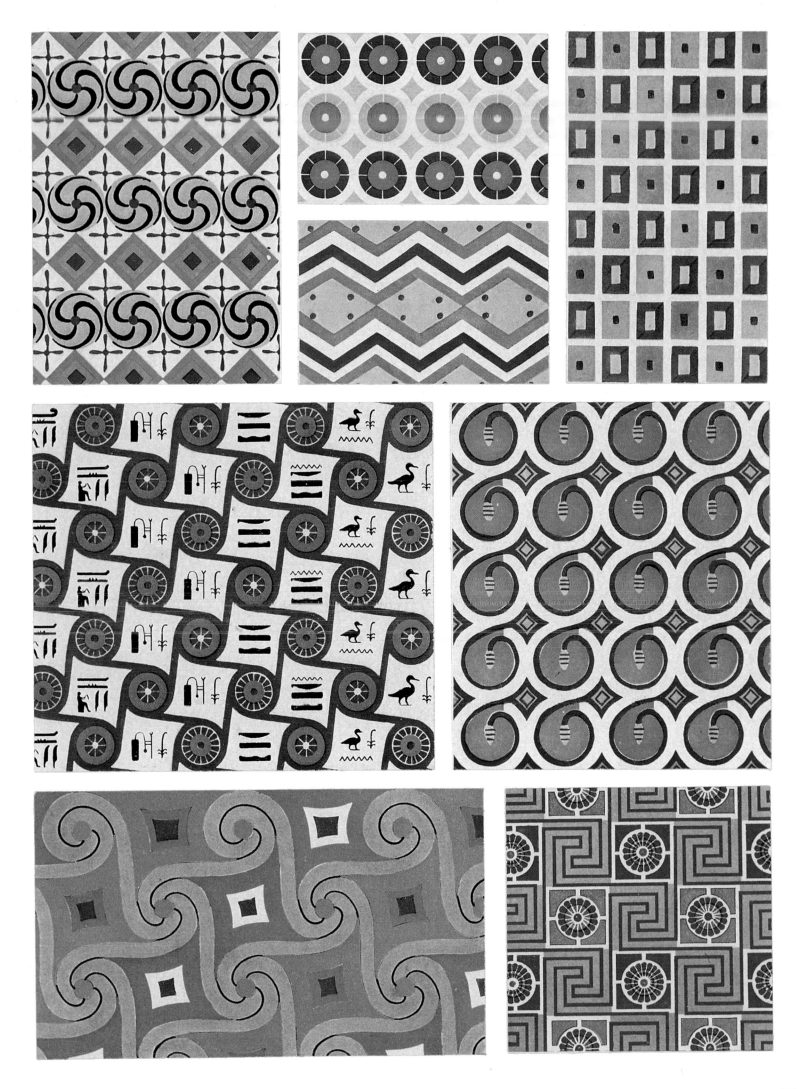

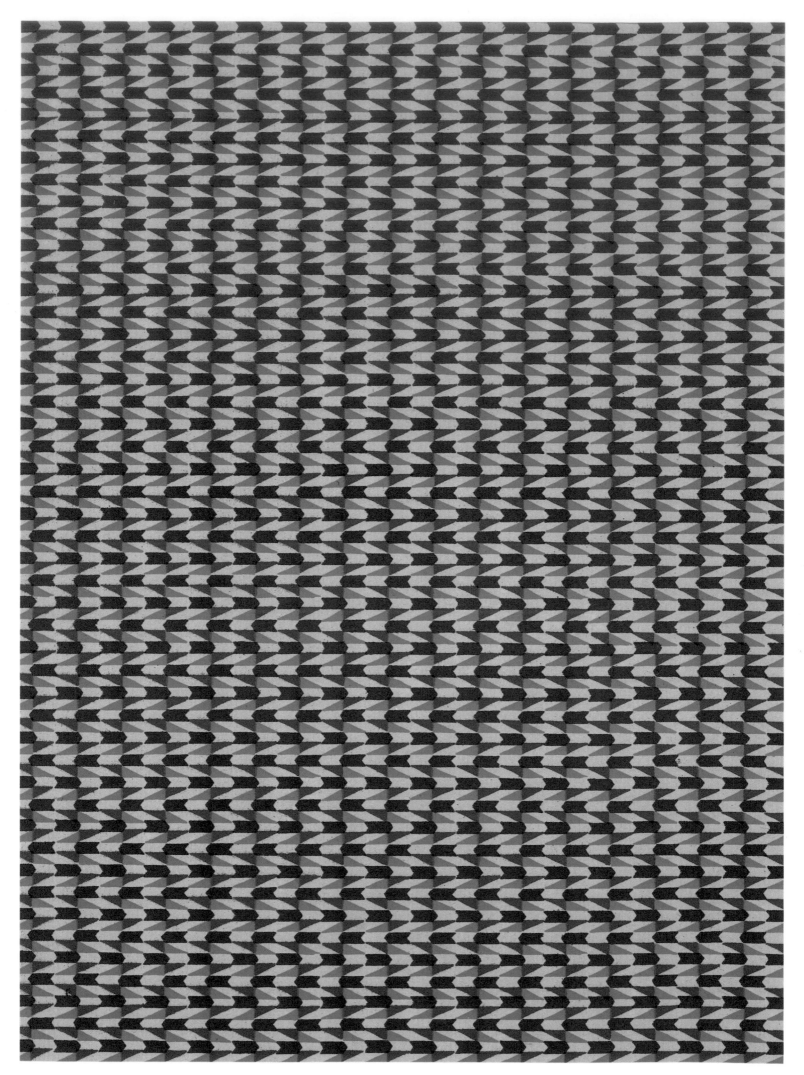

40

41

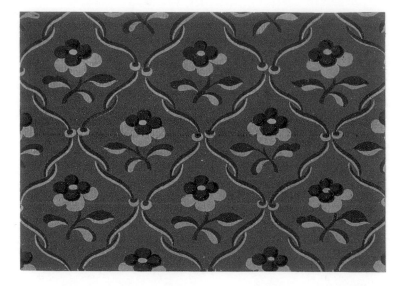

43

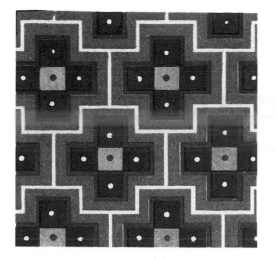

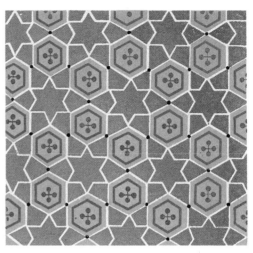
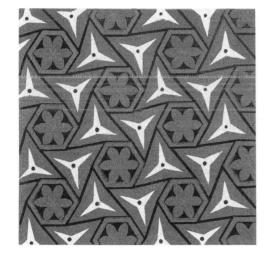

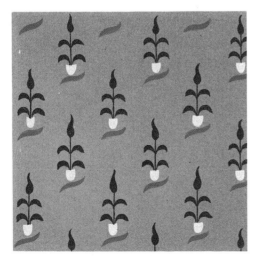

47

48

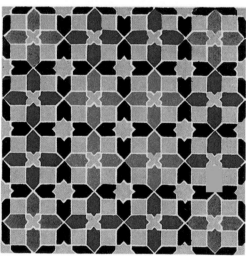

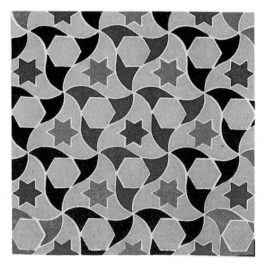

51

52

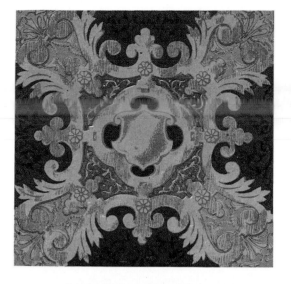

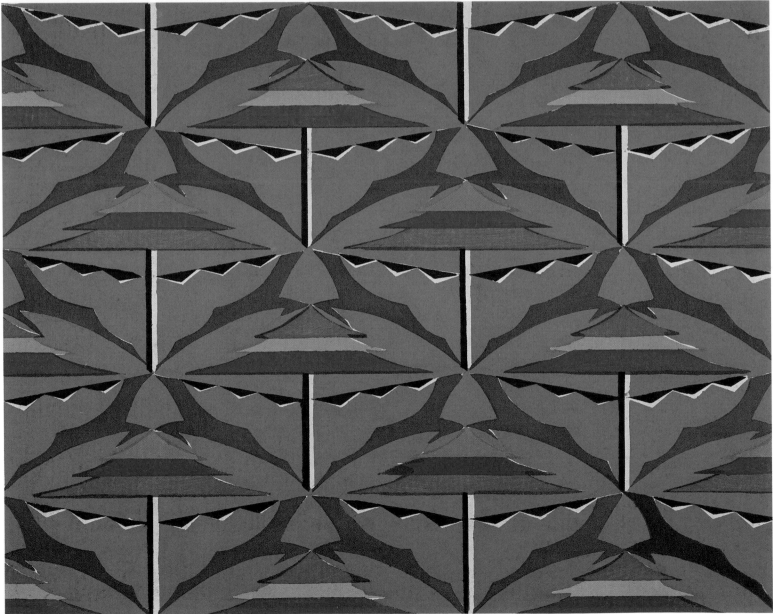

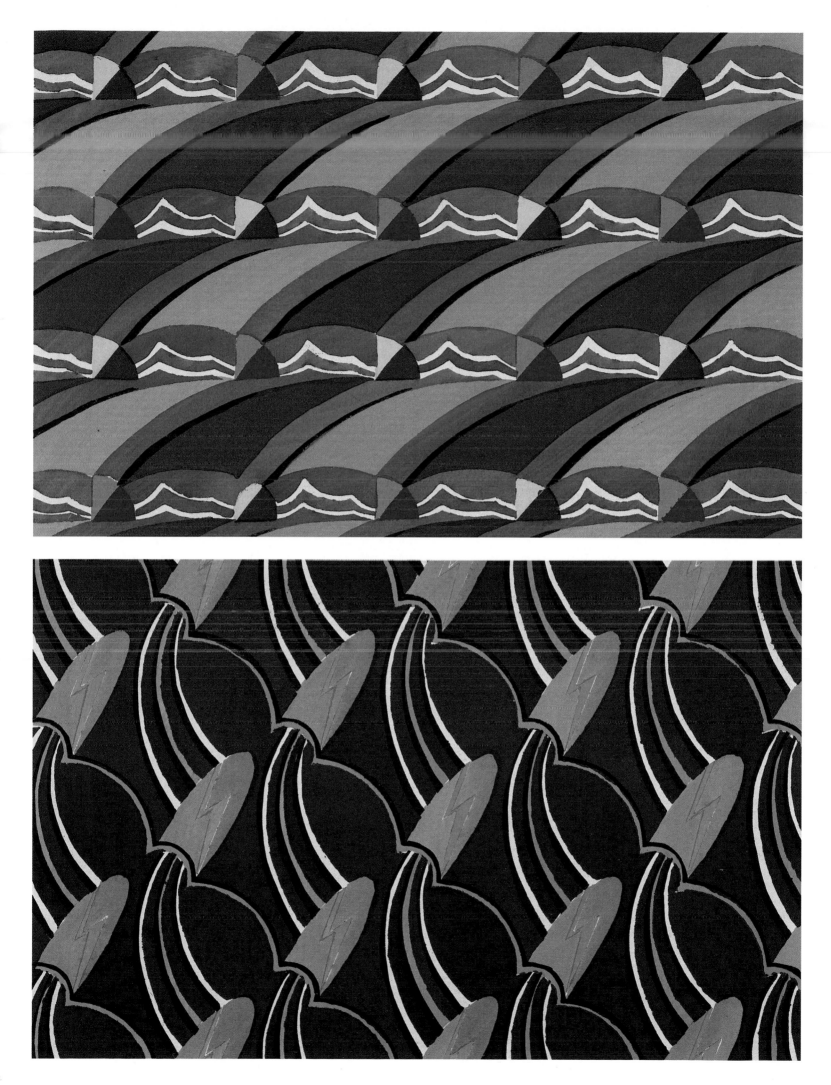

 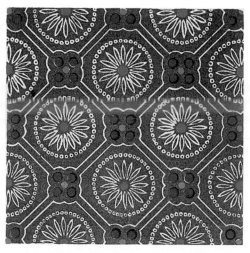 

  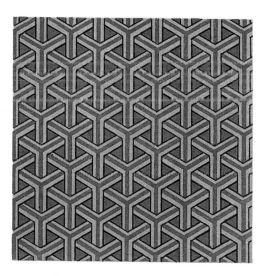

 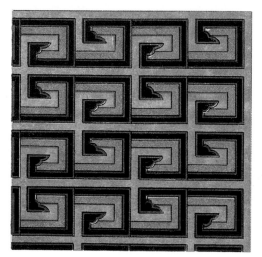 

60

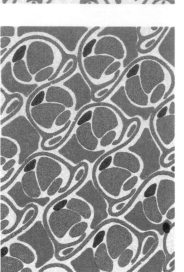

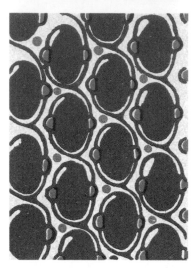

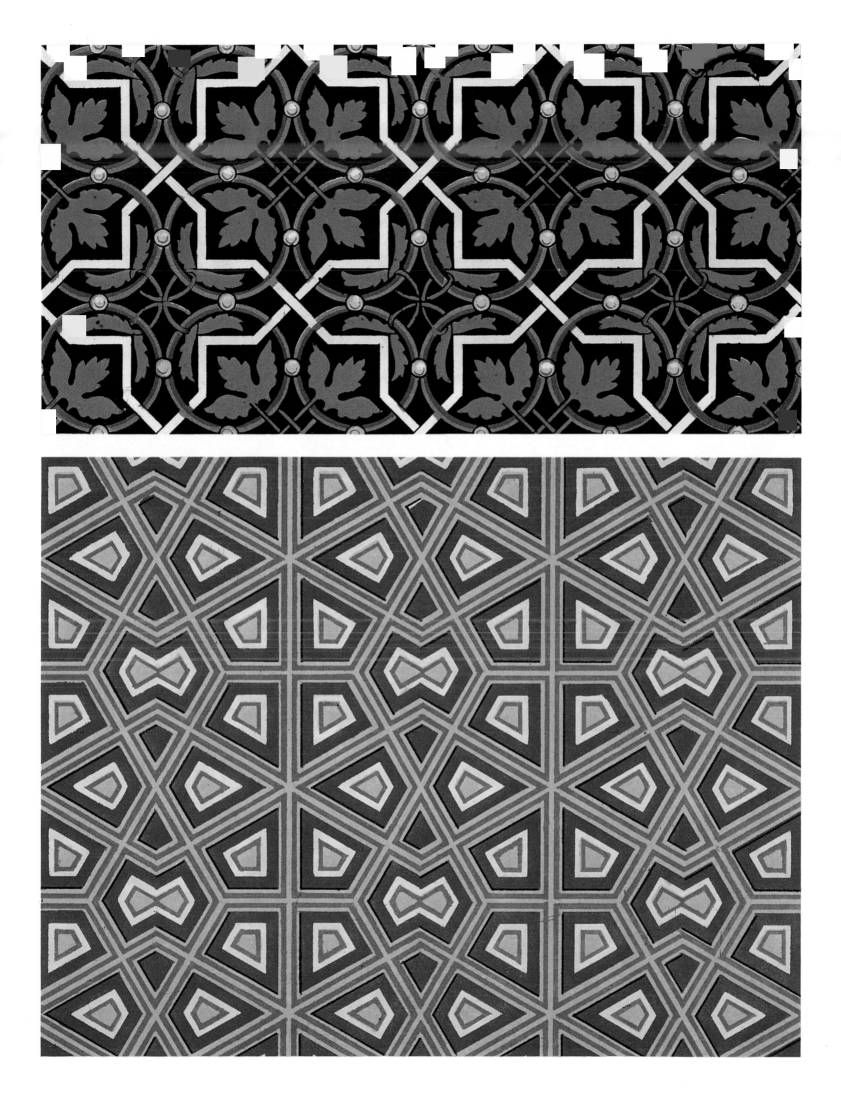

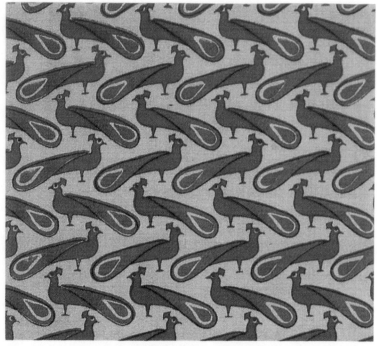

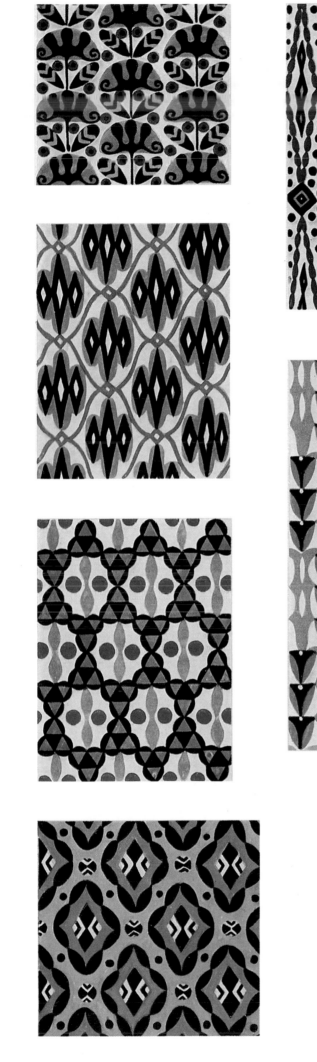

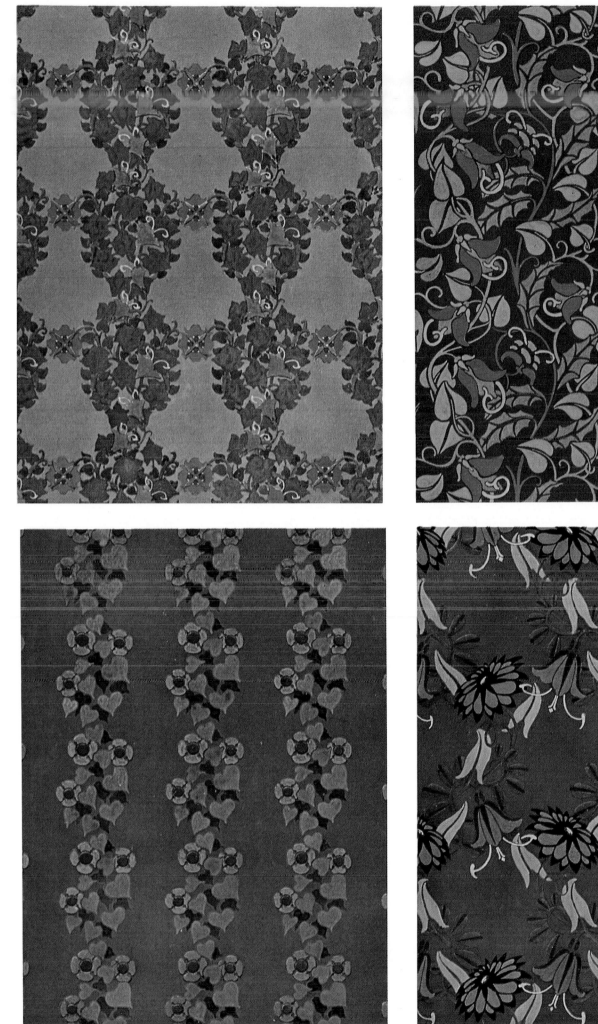

72

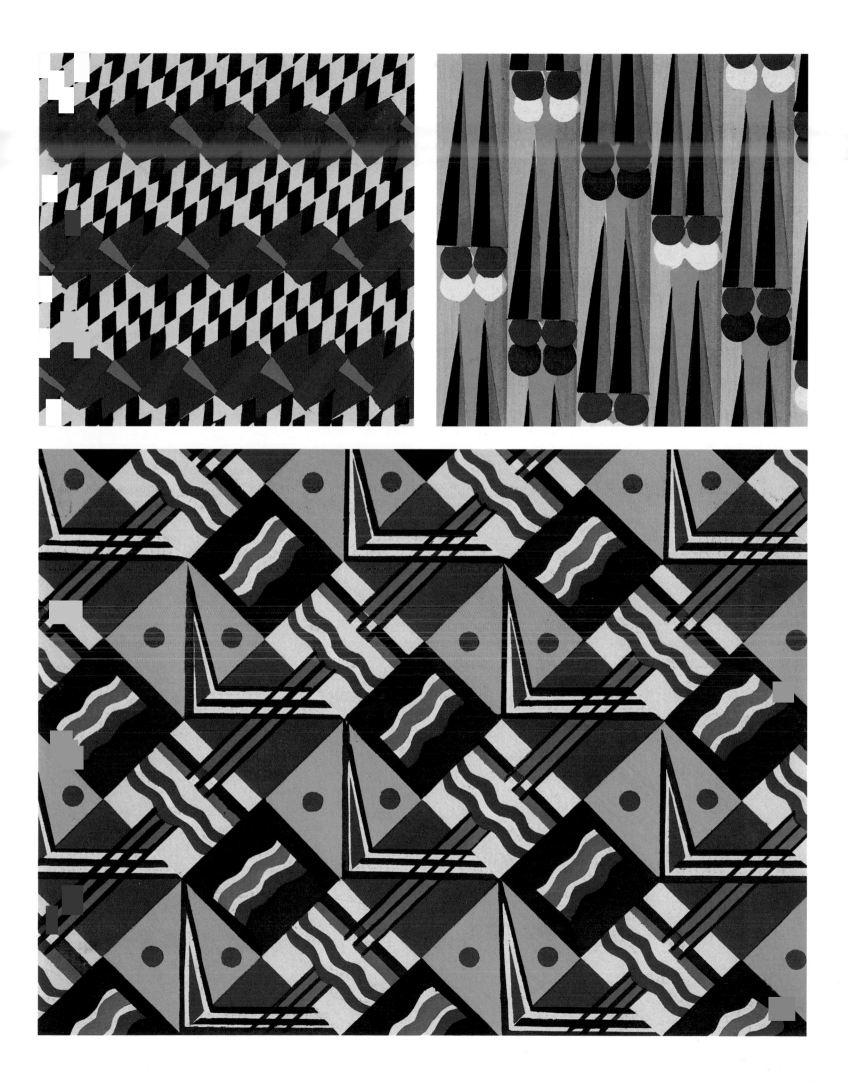

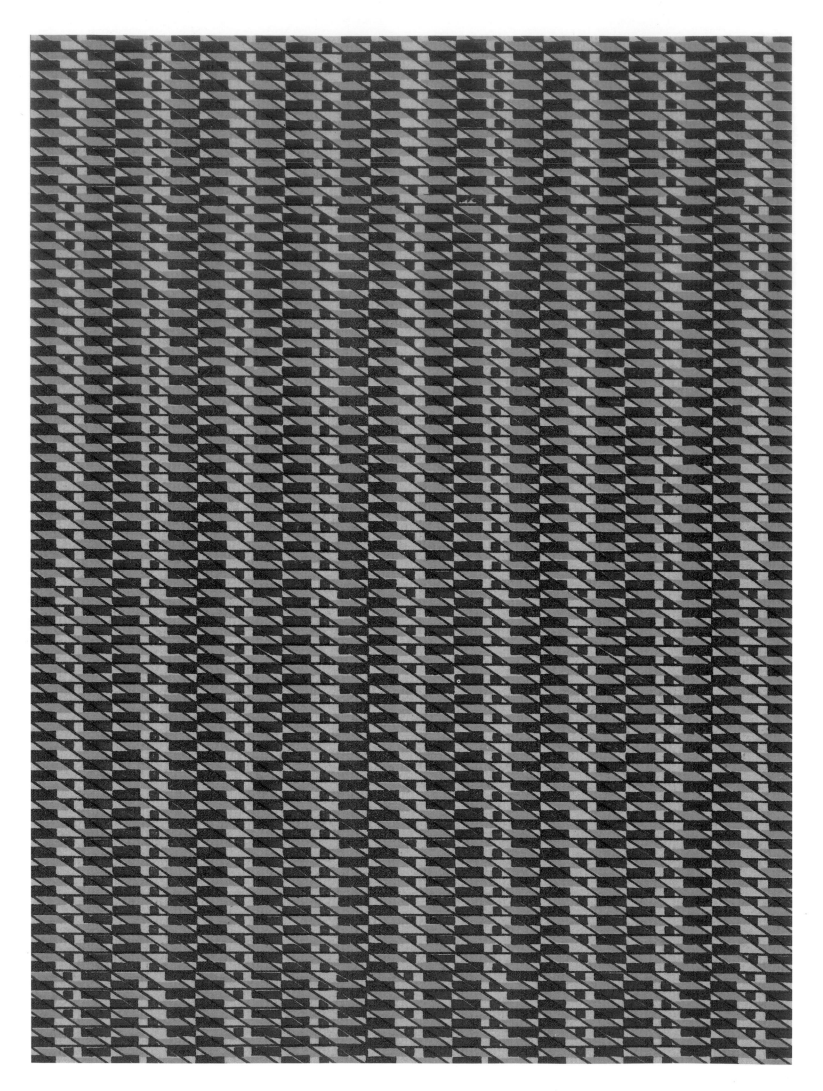

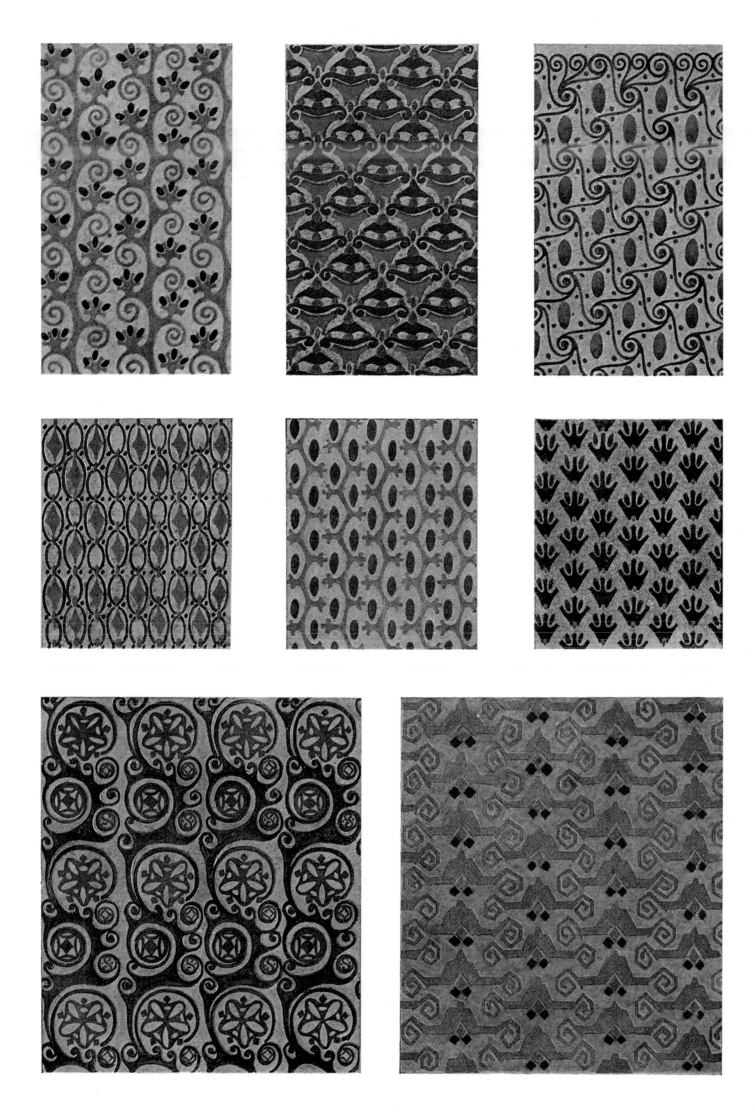

88

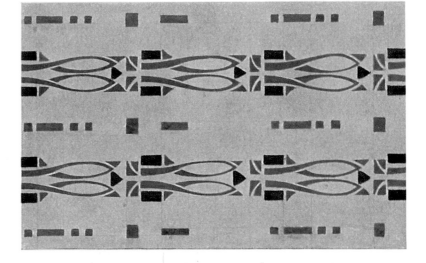

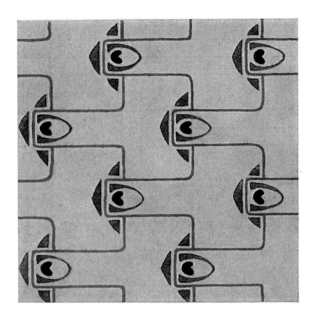

Sources of Designs

Plate

1	Owen Jones. The Grammar of Ornament (London, 1856). Egyptian.
2	Prisse D'Avennes. L'art arabe (Paris, 1885).
3	Tile designs.
4	Friedrich Fischbach. Ornamente der Gewebe (Hanau, ca. 1883).
5	Dekorative Vorbilder. Design by Rudolf Indra.
6	Chinese floral.
7	Moderne Kirchendekorationen.
8	"Kensington Palace." Wallpaper design by Harry Wearne.
9	Dekorative Vorbilder. Design by René Beauclair.
10	Moderne Kirchendekorationen.
11	Dekorative Vorbilder. Design by A. Erdmann.
12	Textile design, 1733.
13	Owen Jones. The Grammar of Ornament (London, 1856). Egyptian.
14	Amish quilt design.
15	Dekorative Vorbilder. Design by Wilhelm Pastern.
16	(top left) Ornamentenschatz. (all others) M. Dupont-Auberville. L'ornement des tissus (Paris, 1877).
17	Dekorative Vorbilder. Design by Hinrikus Feld.
18	Butterflies pattern.
19	Melanges d'Archeologie, 1851.
20	(top left) English wallpaper design, 1905; (top right) William Morris, 1870; (bottom) Lewis F. Day, 1894.
21	(top) Wallpaper design, 1878; (bottom) William Morris, 1872.
22	Wallpaper design, 1795.
23	M. Dupont-Auberville. L'ornement des tissus (Paris, 1877).
24	Friedrich Fischbach. Ornamente der Gewebe (Hanau, ca. 1883).
25	Dekorative Vorbilder. Design by Klasse Josef Hillerbrand.
26	F. Edward Hulme. Suggestions in Floral Design (London, ca. 1880).
27	Friedrich Fischbach. Ornamente der Gewebe (Hanau, ca. 1883).
28	"Carlton House." Wallpaper design by Harry Wearne.
29	Dekorative Vorbilder. Design by A. Zebisch.
30	Arts & Crafts pattern.
31	Dekorative Vorbilder. Design by Georg Kinderman.
32	Art Deco pattern by Serge Gladky, ca. 1929.
33	Kunstgeweberbliche Schmuckformen.
34	George Ashdown Audsley and Maurice Ashdown Audsley. The Practical Decorator and Ornamentalist (Glasgow, 1892).
35	Modern Kirchendekorationen.
36	Friedrich Fischbach. Ornamente der Gewebe (Hanau, ca. 1883).
37	Dekorative Vorbilder. Design by Georg Kinderman.
38	Helmuth Theodore Bossert. Encyclopedia of Colour Decoration. Egyptian.
39	Helmuth Theodore Bossert. Encyclopedia of Colour Decoration. Egyptian.
40	The Curwen Press. Specimen Book of Pattern Papers.
41	(top) Textile design, 1880; (bottom) Owen Jones, 1870.
42	M. Dupont-Auberville. L'ornement des tissus (Paris, 1877).
43	Melanges d'Archeologie, 1851.
44	Persian floral.
45	Owen Jones. The Grammar of Ornament (London, 1856). Persian.
46	Friedrich Fischbach. Ornamente der Gewebe. (Hanau, ca. 1883).
47	Design by William Morris.